First U.S. edition 2014

Library of Congress Catalog Card Number 2014931835

ISBN 978-0-7636-7621-6

14 15 16 17 18 19 TLF 10 9 8 7 6 5 4 3 2

Printed in Dongguan, Guangdong, China

The illustrations in this book were created digitally.

Candlewick Press
99 Dover Street
Somerville, Massachusetts 02144

visit us at www.candlewick.com

CANDLEWICK PRESS

BEFORE

ANNE-MARGOT RAMSTEIN & MATTHIAS ARÉGUI

AFTER

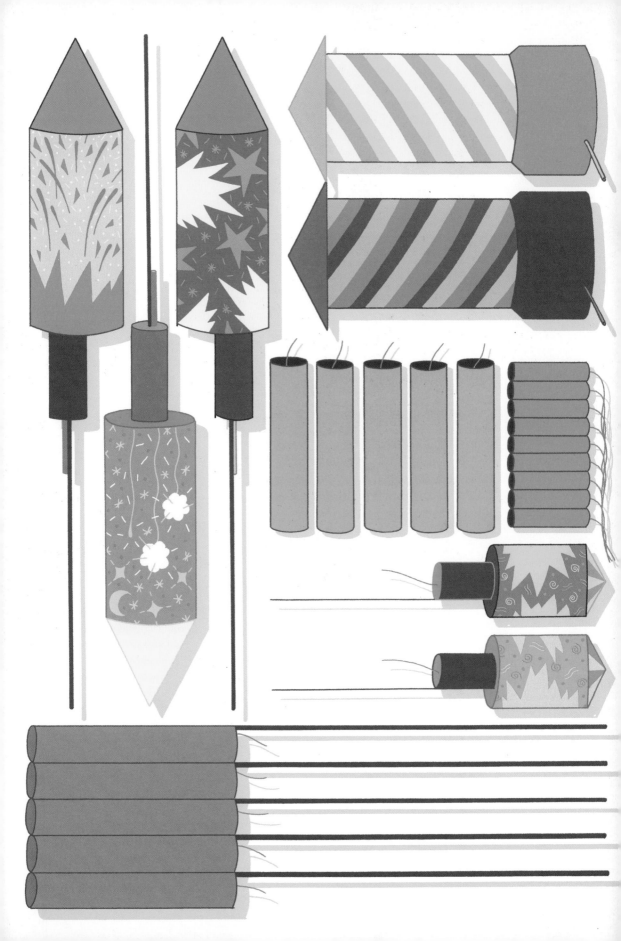

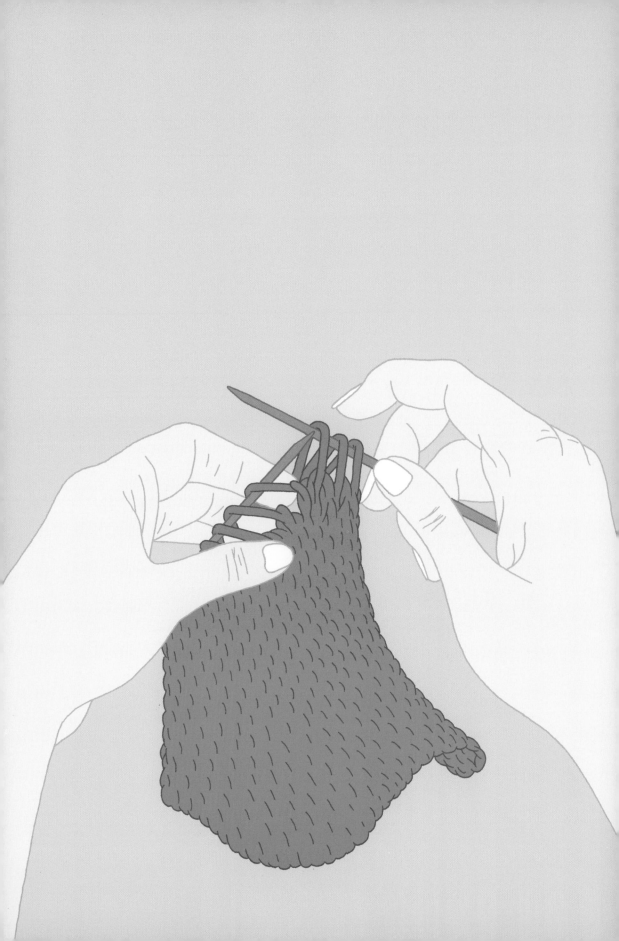

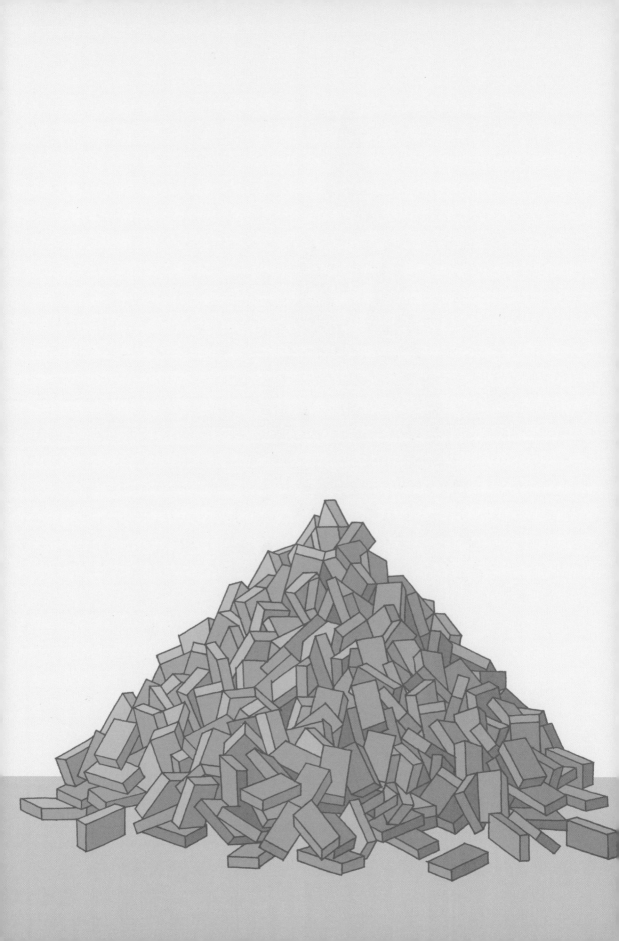

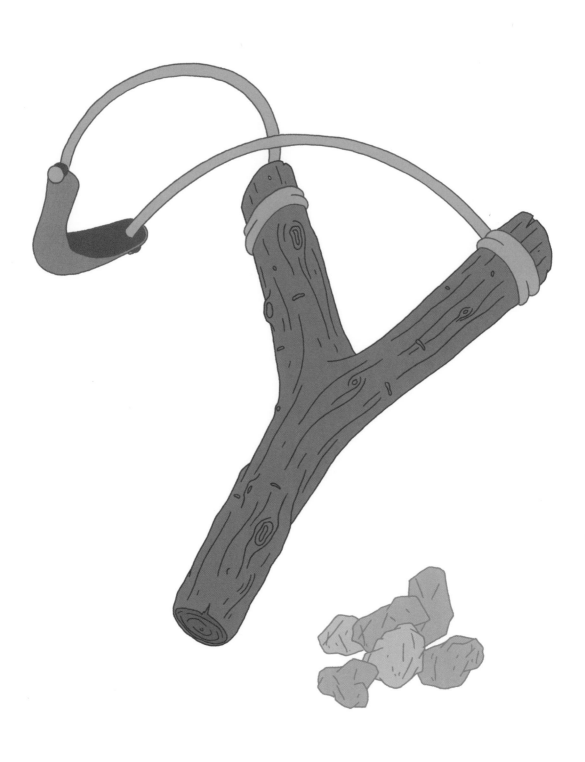

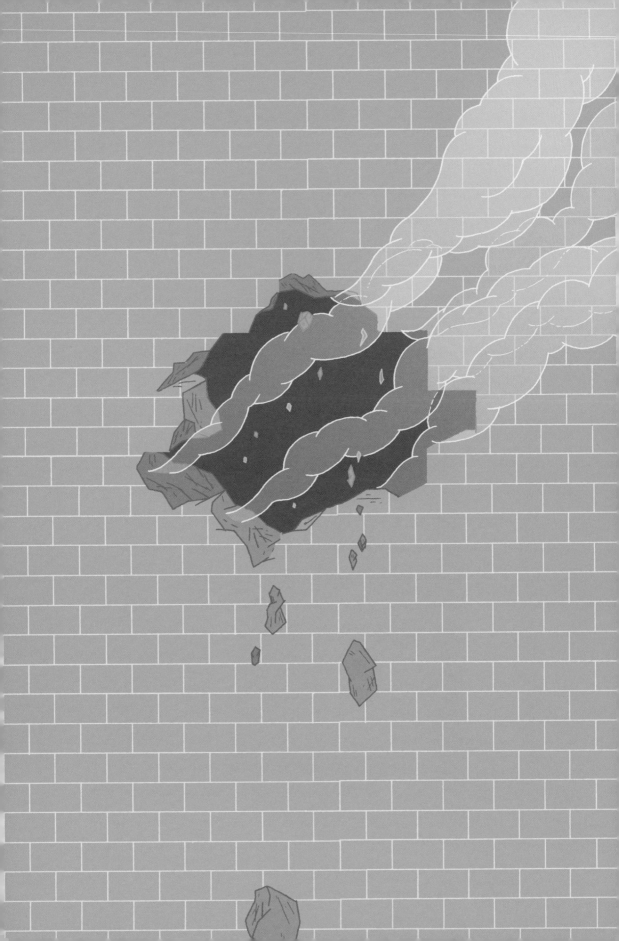

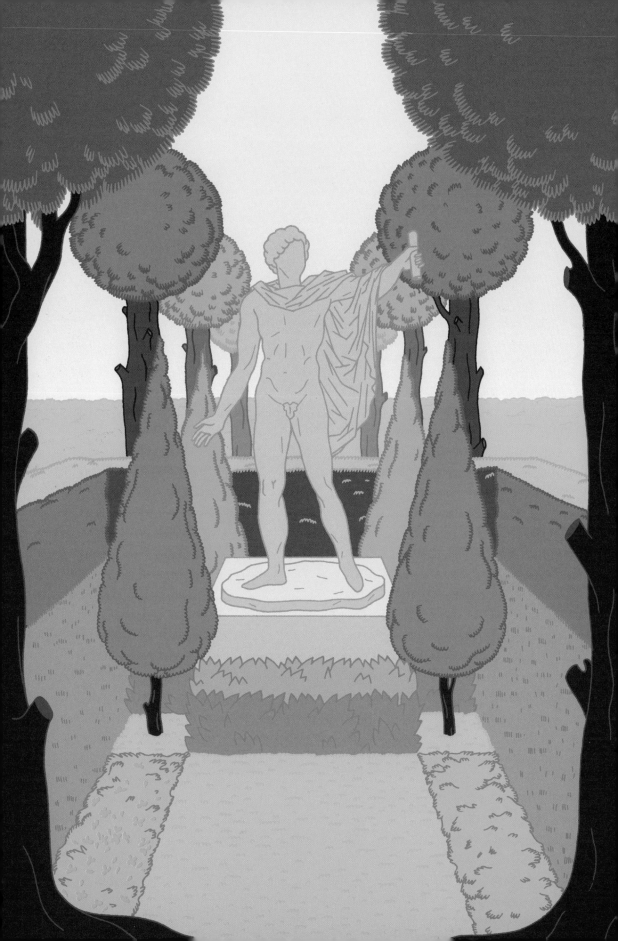

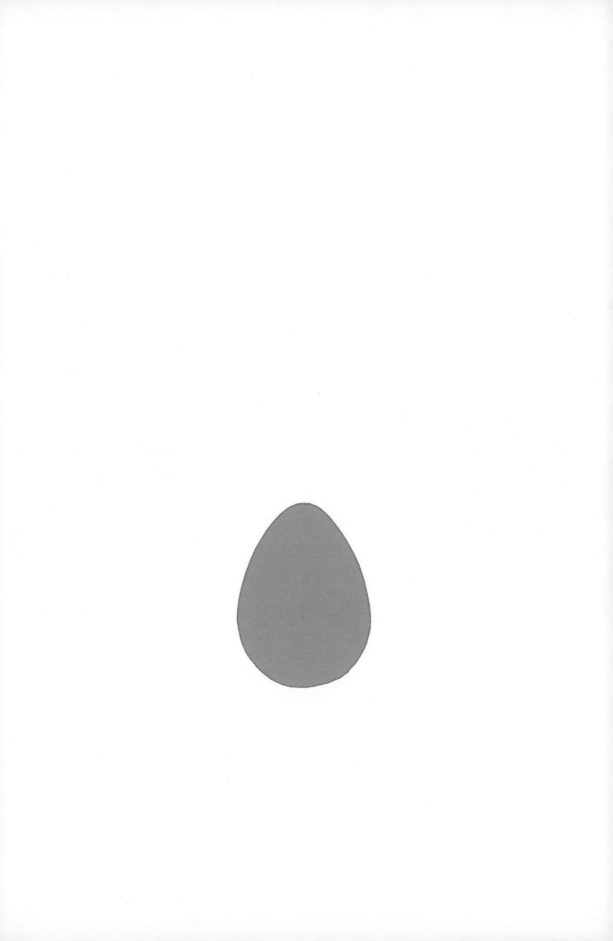

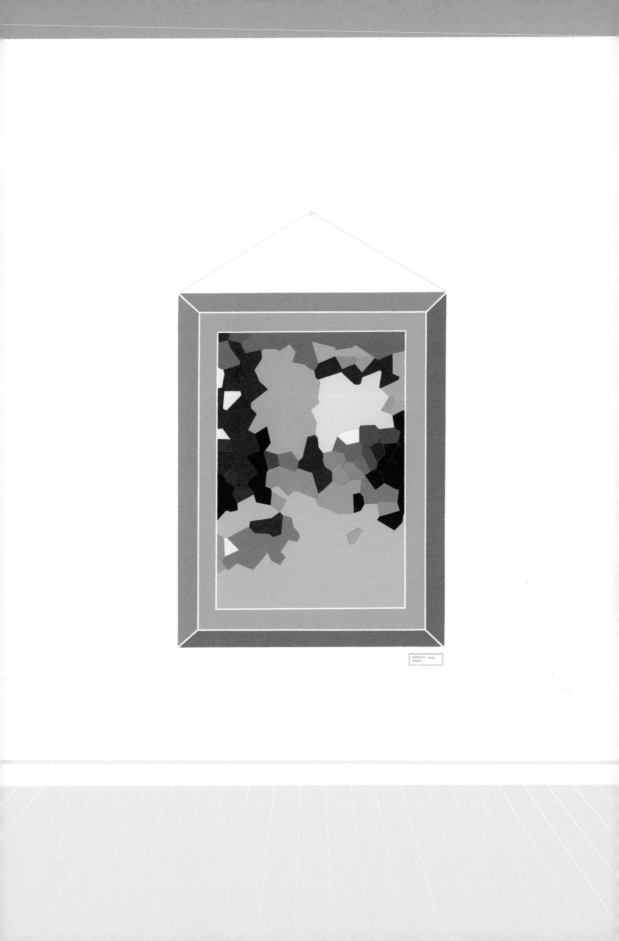

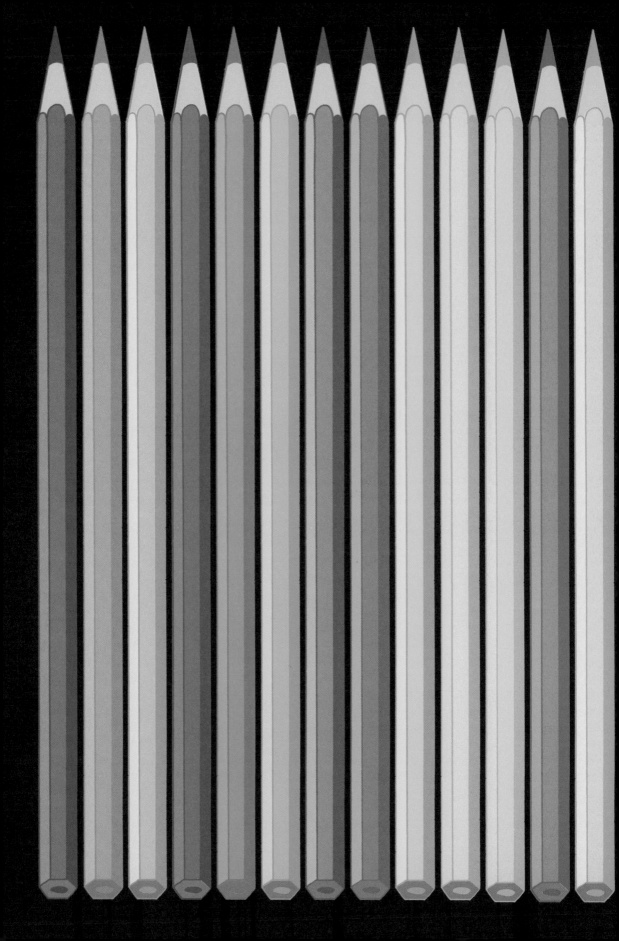

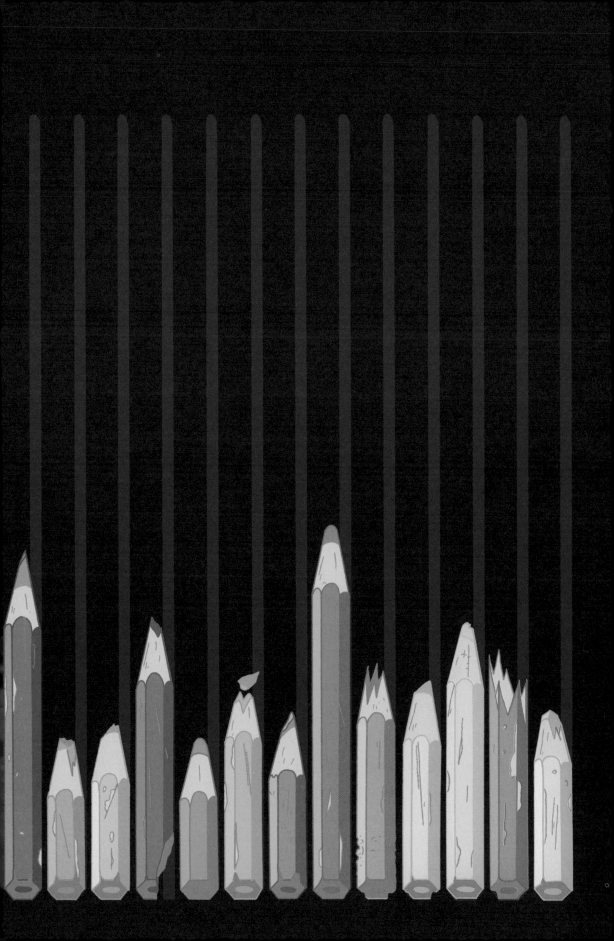

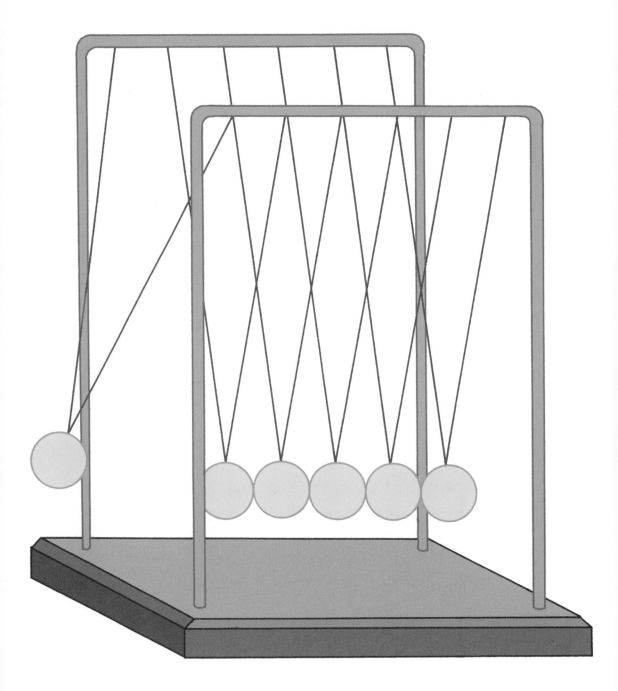

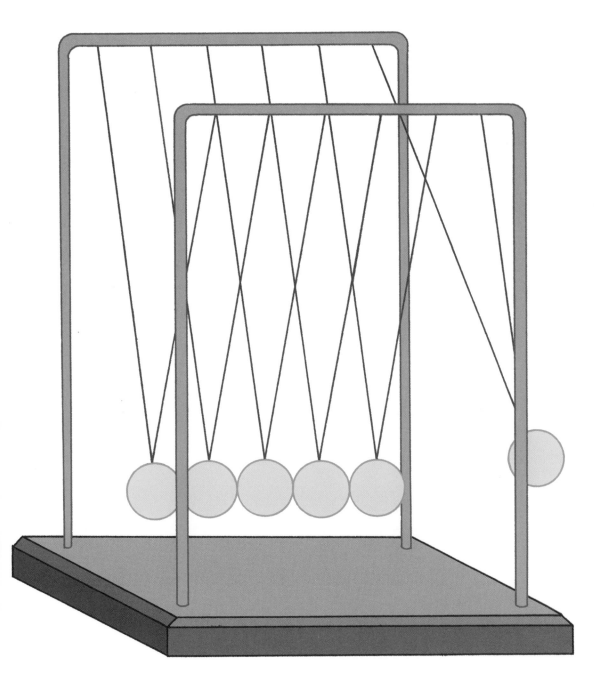

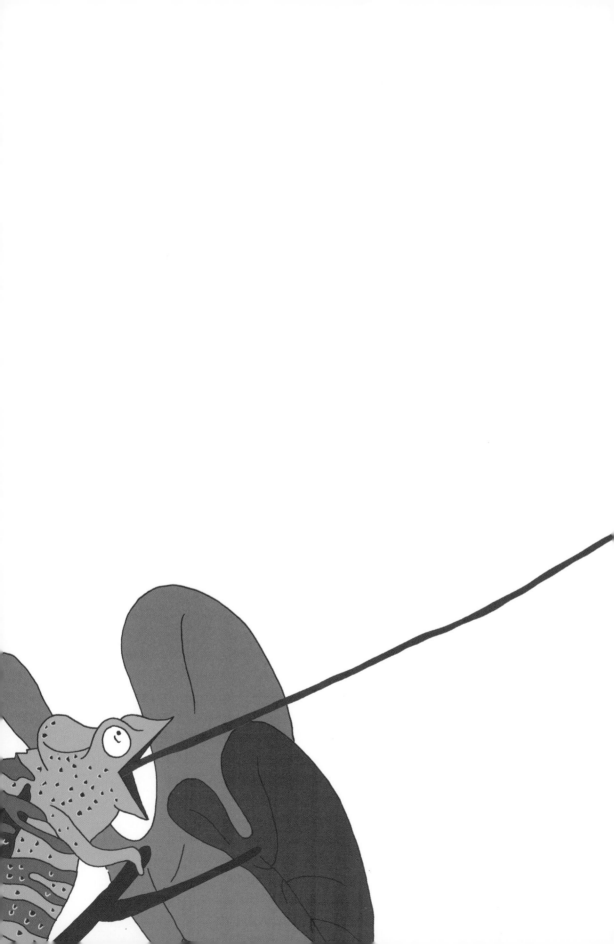

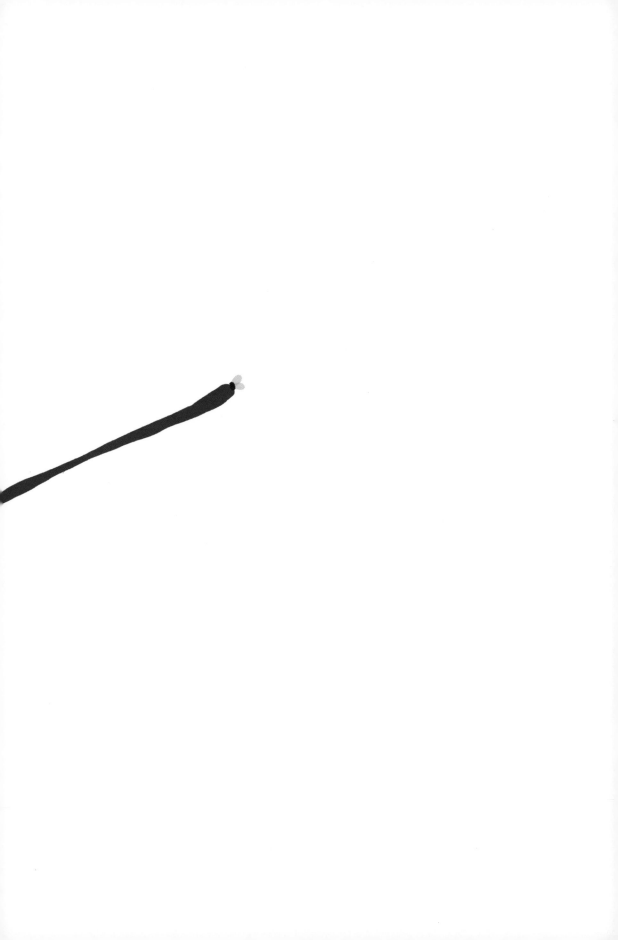

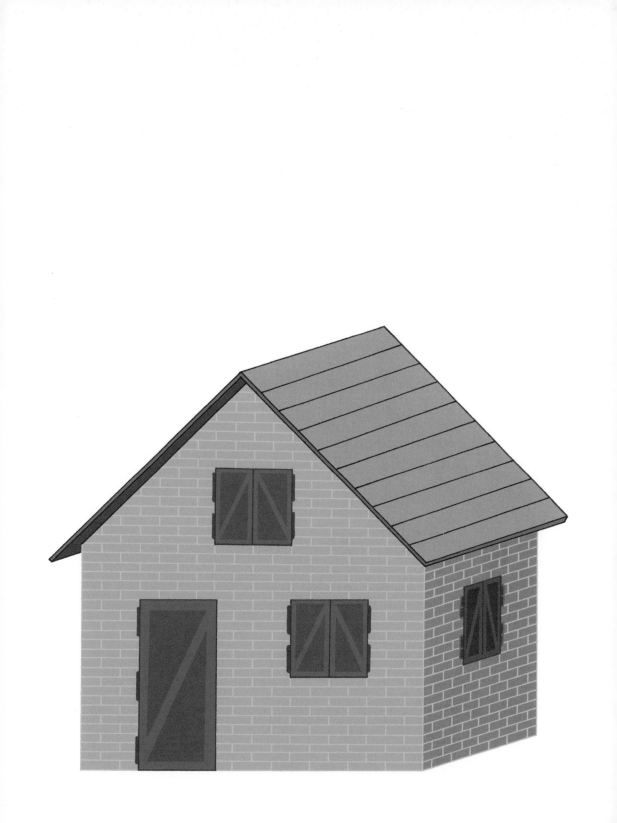

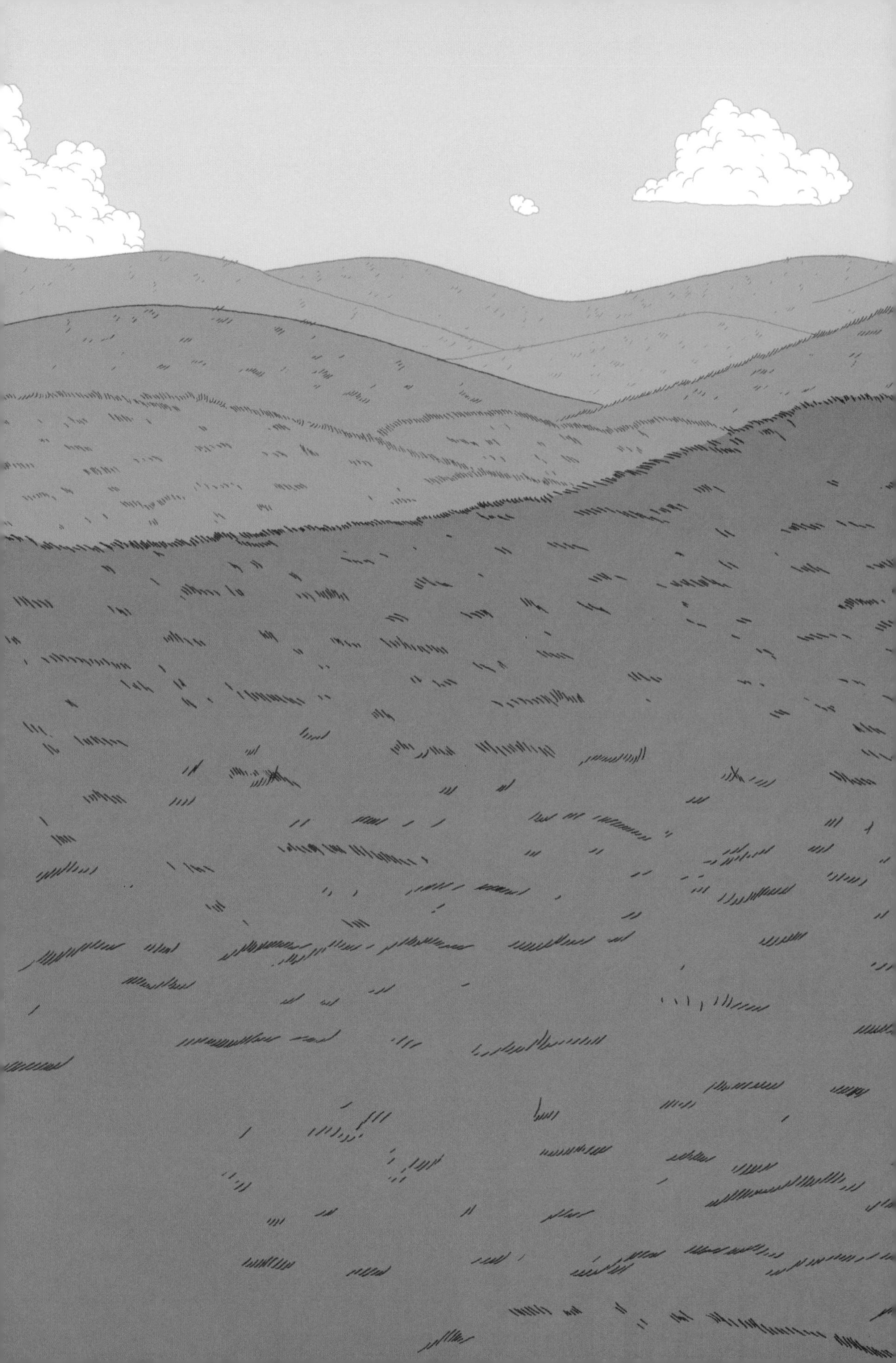

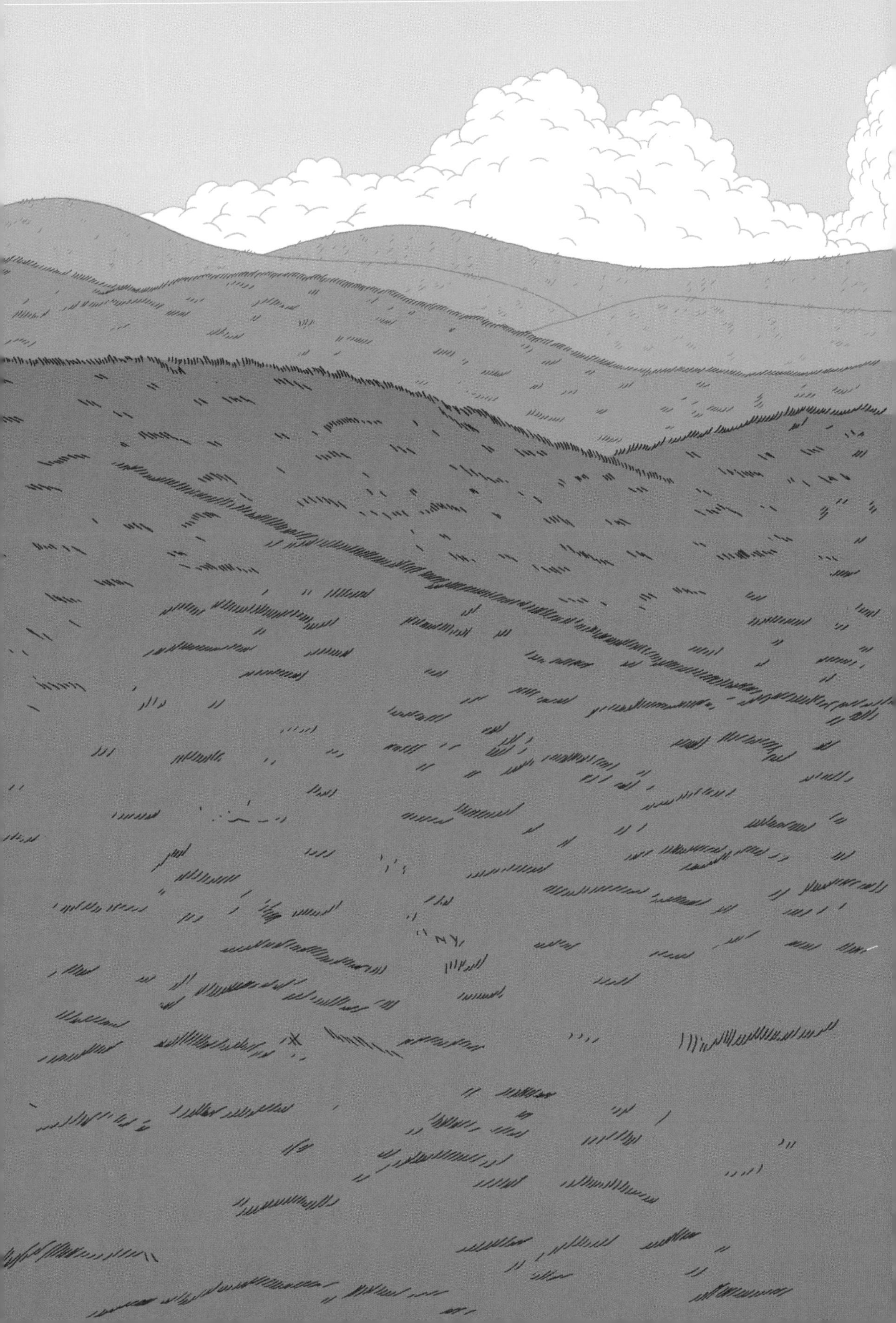

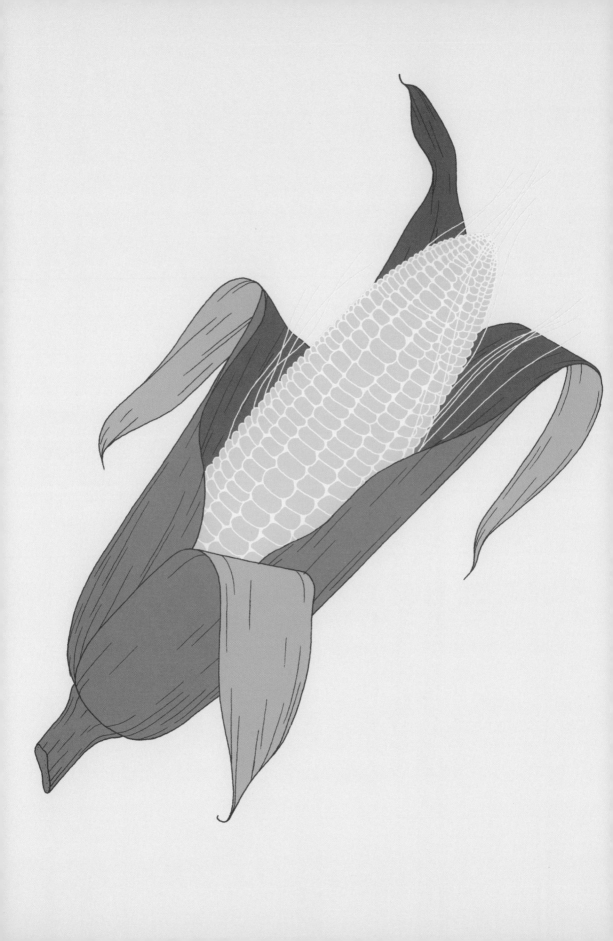

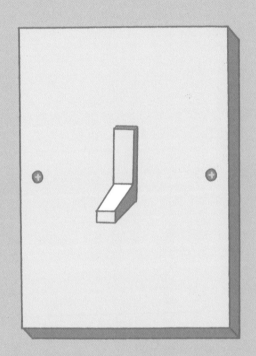